Real-Life
Strange
Encounters

written by Tracey Dils

cover illustration by Jeff Haynie
interior illustrations by Bob Carter

To Trish—
for lending support, creativity, and inspiration

With special thanks to Patricia Houston and Richard
Herrold for reviewing early drafts of these stories and
to Emily H., Kaitlin K., Catie M., Brittany H., Megan T.,
Beth D., and Allison D. for their editorial advice.

PAGES
Publishing Group ™

First printing by Willowisp Press 1998.

Published by PAGES Publishing Group
801 94th Avenue North, St. Petersburg, Florida 33702

Printed in the United States of America

2 4 6 8 10 9 7 5 3 1

ISBN 0-87406-866-5

contents

INTRODUCTION

Imagine you're walking alone at night down a deserted street. A slight glow from the narrow sliver of the moon in the sky provides just a touch of light. Your footsteps sound hollow in the night air.

Then you hear something rustling behind you. At first you think it's just someone's pet dog or cat following you. Then you hear a low growl—and you know it's no pet.

You turn quickly and come face to face with a hideous creature.

A nightmare? Perhaps. But there are many who actually have had close-up encounters with strange beings. History is full of such stories, tales that come from all over the world. Some tell stories of ferocious creatures that seem to take pleasure in hunting down human prey. Others relate stories of gentle, shy creatures who live virtually unnoticed in our world. Still others speak of encounters with creatures who actually help human beings, coming to their rescue in the nick of time.

7

This collection contains retellings of some of the weird and sometimes terrifying encounters people have had with the strange and supernatural. You'll find some classic tales of the Loch Ness monster and the abominable Yeti. You'll find out about someone who met a man-eating tiger up-close and lived to tell about it. You'll read tales of angels, weird space creatures, phantoms, and even a giant squid. And as different as all of these encounters are, they all have one thing in common—they were very real to the people who experienced them.

Did these encounters really happen? That's a question for you, the reader, to answer. I only know that the people who lived to tell about their strange encounters believed that they actually happened—believed them enough to write about the experiences in vivid detail. I have based these stories on their writings.

As a writer, I don't just tell what happened. My job is to tell a good, lively story. As I wrote these stories, I did not change the basic facts of these encounters. Where details were missing, however, I have supplied them. Where dialogue wasn't available, I imagined what the people might have said and wrote it into the stories.

A time may come when you, too, come face to face with something you can't explain. Oh, you might try to use logic to explain it away or you might chalk it up to a vivid imagination. But if you're like these people, you may eventually have to admit what you know to be true— you've just had a strange encounter. And no matter how hard you try to forget about it, the encounter will probably be part of you for years to come.

TERROR at SEA

*F*OR *centuries, sailors have told stories of strange creatures in the sea. They've told tales of beautiful mermaids who captured their hearts with enchanting songs. They've told stories about terrible sea serpents who attacked ships. Legends also exist of huge fish that seem, somehow, to have come from a prehistoric time.*

But one story is so terrifying that only the bravest sailors dare to tell it. It is the story of an encounter with a horrible creature known as the Kraken. During World War II, a group of British soldiers discovered that it was more than just a legend of the sea. It was true—terrifyingly true.

The bloody battle finally ended for the British Army. The Germans had surprised Lieutenant Rolandson and his crew in the South Atlantic. The Germans had fired repeatedly on the British ship and England's Navy just wasn't able to fire back quickly enough. This was one of those short, small battles of World War II that didn't move the Allies any closer to victory. No matter how unimportant the battle, however, the loss of life was, as always, tragic.

Lieutenant Rolandson climbed into a life raft and shook his head sadly. Only Rolandson, two other officers, including his close friend Robert Cox, and nine sailors had survived. And it wasn't likely that they would survive for long on their tiny raft.

The next forty-eight hours were a nightmare. Heat, exhaustion, and thirst overcame the twelve men. The raft had begun to leak and was sinking into the deep, salty water.

Portuguese man-of-wars managed to swim in and out of the raft, stinging the men over and over.

Soon, only five survivors remained. Five of the seven victims died of wounds they had received earlier in the battle. And two men couldn't take the anguish anymore—they jumped from the raft to die in the Atlantic's waters.

Rolandson knew that he had to hang on as long as he possibly could. A rescue mission might have been organized and help could be on its way. He had to keep hoping. It was all he had.

Then the sharks came. They made quick work of the bodies of the dead and began circling the small life raft. Rolandson was truly terrified. The others in the group seemed to be unconcerned, as if they would just as soon be devoured by a shark as to die any other way. But Rolandson could not think of a worse fate.

Suddenly the sharks mysteriously turned and headed the other way. Rolandson breathed a sigh of relief. For the next hour or so, the waters remained calm and peaceful. The man-of-wars didn't bother them. In fact, it seemed as if the entire stretch of ocean had been deserted. For a moment, Rolandson thought this was a sign of his imminent death, that perhaps it was his turn to succumb to the sea's cruel caress.

He looked deep into the ocean waters, awaiting some sign indicating whether he was going to live or die.

And then he saw it—a gigantic shape just under the water. It looked like a huge squid, but it was unlike any sea creature he had ever seen. Each of its tentacles was at least twenty yards long. And its skin was bright red.

"Look!" Rolandson yelled to his companions, sure he was hallucinating. "Do you see it?"

He could tell by the look on Robert's face that he had, indeed, seen the giant creature. He could also tell that the sailor who was sitting just beside him had seen it, too.

The sailor began screaming in terror, yelling the same phrase over and over: "It's the Kraken! The Kraken!"

And before he could yell again, one of the creature's long tentacles smashed into the raft like a giant whip. It grabbed the sailor, wrapping its long arms around him, and began to squeeze him. Rolandson and Robert Cox tried to tear the tentacle away, but they could not stop it.

The long tentacle pulled the sailor, still screaming, into the water.

A few seconds later, the water around the life raft churned a blood red.

Rolandson looked at his fellow survivors. "What was that?" he asked them. "What just happened?"

"It must have been the Kraken," Cox answered. "I thought the stories were just legends, but after what we've just seen . . ."

"The Kraken?" Rolandson asked.

"Yes, you must have heard of it."

"No, I haven't," he said, his voice trembling.

"It's a giant squid, just like the one we saw. The old sailors used to tell stories about it to scare us young ones, you know? They said it always attacks the helpless ones, like us—the ones who aren't going to survive anyway."

"Will it come back?" Rolandson asked.

"Well, it depends," Cox answered. "If we are meant to die, we'll see it again. The Kraken will make short work of us."

Rolandson sat shivering as he pondered what Cox had just told him. It seemed there were no real choices now. He had escaped being killed in the battle and drowning at sea. He had escaped the terror of the shark's bloody attack. And now, if he was to die, it would be the Kraken that would take him—squeezing him to death, and then pulling him into the cold, dark waters that would become his grave.

Neither Rolandson nor Cox slept that night. Though they didn't speak of it, they both watched for the return of the mighty monster, a return that would mean certain death.

The next morning they did see something. But it wasn't the Kraken. It was a Spanish ship. It pulled alongside what was left of the tiny life raft and took the survivors aboard. Rolandson couldn't believe their good fortune.

The ship's doctor took them into his office for an examination. The initial exam went well enough, and the doctor was amazed that they were in such good shape, considering how long they had been adrift.

However, as he examined Rolandson further, he gasped. "You were close to death . . .," he said in broken English.

Rolandson looked up at him in amazement. Neither he nor Cox had told the story of the Kraken. They had figured the Spanish sailors wouldn't believe them. Besides, now that they were rescued, it just didn't seem important anymore.

"What do you mean?" Cox asked.

"The Kraken," the doctor said in barely a whisper and pointed to Rolandson's shoulder.

There, on his back, was a large, round welt—the kind that would have been made by one of the suckers on the creature's tentacles.

The doctor began speaking in rapid Spanish, shaking his head, terror filling his eyes.

Suddenly, he stopped, as if he realized that Rolandson couldn't understand him. Slowly he removed his own shirt. On his shoulder was a round scar, almost identical in size and shape to the one on Rolandson's back.

In that moment, Rolandson grasped the full meaning of what the doctor had said. They had both come close to death—touched by the horrifying Kraken.

THE WOLF BEAST OF GÈVAUDAN

*T*HE *vicious wolf-like beast that stalks and then devours human beings fills the screens of many horror movies. Of course, most people know that such creatures don't really exist.*

Or do they?

In the 1700s French citizens reported tales of a huge, ferocious wolf that attacked innocent children and adults alike. These stories of the wolf's gruesome, bloody carnage were more frightening than any make-believe horror story.

What exactly was this huge wolf-like beast? What caused his vicious behavior? And why did it choose to terrorize the people of the French countryside? Historians and scientists have never been able to answer these questions.

Two, more terrifying questions need to be answered, as well: Was there only one beast of Gèvaudan? If there was more than one, as many suspected, how many more could be out there, waiting to kill again?

Antoine de Beauterne had been given a strange commission. As the French king's personal gunman in the 1700s, he was used to carrying out the king's bidding. Antoine had participated in fox hunts, had trained the king's army, and had helped prepare France for battle, should the nation ever be attacked.

But he never expected to be asked to hunt down and kill some vicious wolf-like beast. The description of the beast was horrible—almost too horrible to be true. In fact, it sounded as if the stories of the beast had come from some gruesome version of a fairy tale.

Still, Antoine knew the seriousness of his task as he approached the village of Gèvaudan in the French Alps. Reports described a bloody spring in this small country town. As usual, the adults had sent the older peasant children into the rugged mountains surrounding the town to tend to the sheep and cattle. As was the custom, the children spent several days at a time there, bringing food, sleeping rolls, and other provisions with them in small packs. It had been a way of life in this part of France for several centuries.

Only this year, some of the children didn't come back.

One girl was found in a low green valley, beside a stream. Her heart had been completely torn from her chest.

A young boy was found the next week in an isolated field. His throat had been viciously attacked, and he had been left to die of his bloody wound.

Soon, a kind of hysteria grew in the village. The people no longer allowed their children to go outdoors, much less into the mountains. The people left the livestock untended in the field. And, as the townspeople cowered in terror, more reports of the beast kept coming.

Apparently, the wolf-beast had devoured an

old woman in the next town. It had killed a little boy who had been out playing with his sister. It had carried off a small child who had been sleeping in the shade of the trees.

And the word spread, not only to the king's court in France, but to neighboring countries as well. France soon became the mockery of nearby countries, especially England. France was too weak to protect its own people, the Englishmen said. Others said that the entire country would be destroyed by this legendary beast. The embarrassment was too much for the king to bear; therefore, he summoned Antoine to take care of the problem once and for all.

Antoine had been in Gèvaudan only a few hours when the townspeople, having heard of his mission, began knocking at the door of his room at the town's only inn.

A peasant woman came calling first, telling an outrageous tale of how she had come face to face with the beast and had lived, in spite of the encounter. She claimed to have seen the beast in the fields by her home. It walked on two legs, she said, like a human being, but its body was covered with rust-colored hair and it had a snout like a pig. It was as big as a donkey and had a long, bushy tail. The beast had scared off her dogs, the woman went on. There were a couple of cows grazing in her field, though, and one of them had used its horns to attack the beast. She said that the beast had taken off into the woods and had not bothered her since.

Next, a priest knocked on his door, saying that the beast was surely a messenger of evil, sent to punish the people for their sins. A few peasants followed, claiming that witchcraft was involved and that the wolf was a human who somehow was being transformed into a beast.

The stories sounded fantastic, even laughable, to Antoine. He was sure the creature was no more than an ordinary wolf and that the townspeople had allowed their imaginations to create preposterous tales.

Antoine spent three months preparing for the hunt. He tried to learn all he could about the area and the beast. Then he drew maps, took short hikes around the town, and investigated the places where people claimed to have seen the creature. During those three months no additional attacks had happened, but the people still talked about the creature and they stayed indoors, allowing their livestock to roam free in the hills.

One day Antoine received word from the king. The king wanted Antoine to do something soon. Rumors about the beast were running out of control. Antoine needed to organize the hunt before word spread any further.

On a warm day in September, Antoine gathered together forty local hunters and twelve dogs. They headed from the village to a ravine where the beast had been sighted several times. He ordered some of the men to circle the ravine. With several of the more-trusted men, Antoine positioned himself at one side of a wide clearing. Then the men began banging the underbrush with clubs and sticks and blowing their horns. At the same time, they tightened the circle. If the beast was there, Antoine had told them, the noise would force it out.

The men drew the circle tighter and tighter. Then the dogs began barking excitedly.

The men unleashed the dogs. Antoine's heart beat hard. The dogs sensed something was there, but what?

Suddenly, a wolf-like beast ran into the

opening. It was much like the woman had described it: a huge wolf, but it walked on all fours instead of on two legs as she had claimed. Its fur was deep reddish-brown and was matted in places. Its eyes glowed a blood red. Antoine gasped as it opened its mouth and snarled at the dogs and men in front of it. White foam hung from its fangs.

Then it turned wildly as if it suddenly realized it was trapped. His hands shaking, Antoine shouldered his gun and fired. The bullet hit the beast in its right shoulder. It fell, rolled back and forth in the dirt for a few seconds, and then lay still on the ground.

Antoine approached cautiously, wanting to be sure the animal was dead. From behind him, the other men walked slowly toward the creature.

Suddenly, the creature rose up! It reared high in the air, growling a deep guttural growl. Then it lunged at Antoine. Just as the beast slashed its sharp claws toward Antoine's neck, another shot rang out. The bullet hit the beast in the thigh. It collapsed to the ground once again.

This time the men didn't stop firing. They shot the creature three times in the head to ensure its death.

Upon closer inspection, the men discovered that the creature was indeed a type of wolf, an enormous dog-like animal measuring about six feet from nose to tail. Its head was huge and each of its fangs was about an inch and a half long. Crying, "The beast is dead, the beast is dead," the men carried the animal into Gèvaudan, where the people gathered around and cheered.

Antoine had the creature stuffed and he returned with it to the king's court. The countryside was declared safe for the people, especially for the children, once again.

But that was not the last Gèvaudan would hear of the beast. The countryside was quiet for a time, until the cold winds of December set in. It was then that a young girl named Julienne Denis disappeared. Her brother reported that she had been behaving strangely. Even though the beast had been killed, she kept insisting that it still lived and that it would someday overcome her. In fact, she had become so terrified of the beast that it was all she seemed to talk about. No amount of comfort would ease her mind.

Then, suddenly, she stopped talking about the animal—in fact, she stopped speaking completely. She became deeply troubled and would simply stare off into space as if she was in a trance. Then one icy night, she slipped out of the house completely unnoticed.

A week later they found what was left of her. Some bones, rags, and a few traces of her hair were found beside an icy stream. The snow around the grisly remains of her body was stained with her blood.

Her brother was sure it was the work of the beast once again—a different beast to be sure, but a beast all the same. And this one was even more evil and treacherous than the last. He swore revenge on the creature. He was going to make sure this creature was dead once and for all.

A number of the townspeople feared that the beast had returned to plague them once again, so they joined him in his hunt. One, a Jean Chastel, was reluctantly accepted by the band of hunters. He was a strange man. He lived almost like a wild animal himself in a small shack in the woods. But the revengeful brother accepted his help and was intrigued by

Chastel's knowledge of the creature. Chastel claimed that the creature wasn't just a wild beast, but instead was the image of evil itself. There was only one way to rid the country of this ferocious wild creature, Chastel claimed. It had to be killed with a silver bullet. And he loaded his gun with two of them just to be sure.

Once again, the hunters brought their dogs and their clubs. They formed a circle as Antoine had shown them and pounded the ground near the spot where Julienne's remains had been found in the snow. They pounded for more than three hours. But strangely, Chastel didn't join them in their pounding. Instead, he read prayers loudly from his prayer book, his gun at the ready by his side.

Suddenly, just as the men where about to give up and move to another area, there was a rustling sound. The dogs began barking, straining at their leashes. The men let them go and they ran to a patch of low bushes.

In a flash, a wolf-shaped animal, this one bigger than before, leapt from the shadows. The beast bared its fangs, which this time dripped with blood. Its eyes were a hideous yellow. As soon as the beast appeared, an overpowering stench of decay filled the air.

Julienne's brother was amazed when Chastel stood by calmly, refusing to acknowledge the creature in front of him. Chastel finished his prayer as the creature growled at the dogs. Then he put the book aside and raised his rifle.

A single shot rang out. The silver bullet pierced the animal's forehead, right between its eyes. As the beast fell to the ground, Chastel simply said, "Good has overcome. You will kill no more."

No such beasts were seen in the French countryside ever again. No one, not even Chastel himself, could explain what the beast was or where it had come from. And no one really knew if just two beasts had existed, or if several of them were still hiding in the hills. The townspeople of Gèvaudan did know one thing: Chastel had been right. The beast was an incredibly evil animal. But a silver bullet—and the power of Chastel's prayers—finally killed the creature.

Only one grisly reminder lingered.

The spot where the beast fell dead remained

bare. A large dusty spot, shaped like the beast's body, could be seen in the field where it had died. Although many tried to make grass grow there, the earth seemed to be forever fouled and refused to yield life where the beast had died its horrible death.

YETI

*H*IGH in the Himalayan Mountains, some claim, lurks a huge ape-like creature that has struck terror in the local natives and explorers alike. The tough Sherpa people who inhabit the region call it "Yeti," and they tell spine-tingling tales of encounters with the beast. They even warn their children of the Yeti, cautioning them to run downhill if they ever meet the creature. They claim this is the best chance of escape because the awkward

*creature's hair will fly in his face and he will fall
down in the snow.*

*Reportedly, British explorers have come face
to face with Yeti. Because of his similarity to a
snowman, they began to call him the "Abominable Snowman." Some of the braver adven-
turers have actually tracked the Yeti. One claims
to have found a Yeti scalp. Another tells the
story of discovering a family of the creatures in a
tree-covered lair.*

*Of course, some doubt that the Yeti really
exists. Sir Edmund Hillary himself, the first to
conquer Mount Everest, scoffs at the tales.
However, other respected explorers insist that
they have seen him. And one of these explorers,
William Knight, got a clear look at the Yeti. If it
had been any closer, though, Knight might never
have lived to tell his tale.*

William Knight had traveled a long way to
reach this remote spot on the Tibetan plateau.
His journey had taken him through the deserted wilderness, over ice-covered fields, and
up the sides of tall mountains. His guides were
the tough natives of Nepal. Known as Sherpas,
they did more than just show him the way.

They carted his gear, helped him make his camp, and cooked his meals. They didn't share the same language or the same country, but Knight did share with them a sense of awe and respect for the natural world.

They were tough people, these Sherpas, but they were gentle, too. Knight discovered that they were also very superstitious. They believed that certain routes were bad luck and they often took the more difficult way to avoid any disasters. As they moved along, the Sherpas kept looking over their shoulders as if they were afraid of being followed. Occasionally, Knight heard them speak the same word over and over. It sounded like "yeddi" or "yeti." Knight figured it was probably some sort of good luck charm.

Since the beginning of the journey, the Sherpas had rarely left Knight alone, which annoyed him somewhat. Part of what he liked about being out in the wilderness was the chance to be alone. Absolute solitude—that's what Knight was looking for. He needed time away from his busy life in London. But he had had precious little time alone on this trip.

The sun was just setting as they reached

the top of the plateau. Knight gestured to the Sherpas to go ahead of him. He decided to stay for just a moment to survey the splendor that lay before him. The Sherpas protested, saying that strange "yeddi" word again.

"Go, go!" Knight said, waving them on in the hope that they would understand. "Make camp," he said, making gestures to indicate what he wanted them to do. "I will join you by and by."

The Sherpas looked reluctant, even a bit fearful, but they followed his instructions and headed toward the center of the plateau where they had planned to make camp.

Knight stood and watched the glint of the sun as it reflected off the snowy fields. The sight before him was simply incredible. The grandeur of the scene made him feel as if all of his problems were small and insignificant— just as he was in this great expanse.

And then Knight saw something on the horizon.

It looked like a large brown speck—some sort of animal perhaps. It moved ever so slowly on the edge of a snow-covered field.

"That's odd," Knight said to himself. "There

aren't many animals of that size at this altitude."

Knight pulled out his field glasses and focused them on the brown speck.

What he saw amazed him. A huge ape-like creature, covered in a kind of yellow fur with a shock of dark hair on its head, moved slowly against the snowy background. As Knight later wrote, "The muscular development in his arms, thighs, legs, and chest was terrific. He had in his hand what seemed to be some form of a primitive bow."

Knight watched, spellbound. The creature seemed unaware of him. Instead, it was focused on something else on the other side of the hill, perhaps a smaller animal that would be his prey. Knight squinted to see through the field glasses, trying to get a good look at the creature's face.

Then Knight heard a shrill scream from just ahead of him.

It was one of the Sherpas. "Yeti!" the man screamed and he quickly scrambled down the embankment.

The creature below must have heard him, because it raced down the hill at an incredible speed.

The Sherpa grabbed Knight roughly.

"What is the meaning of this?" Knight asked.

But the Sherpa was forceful. He threw Knight over his shoulder and carried him up toward camp.

Later, when he returned to the base camp, Knight learned more about what he had seen. The creature, an interpreter explained, had been the fearsome Yeti that the Sherpas had been chanting about. Though incredible, the Sherpa people had told stories about the loathsome creature for years. Some said that the Yeti had been known to attack children, stealing them from their homes. The Yeti had also been blamed for the deaths of many Sherpa guides, not to mention a few English explorers as well.

But his blood grew cold when he heard the last fact about the Yeti: The Sherpas claimed that if a person looked at the Yeti's face, that person would die a horrible, painful death.

That was what the Sherpa guide had been trying to tell Knight. Although Knight was never sure whether he had been facing imminent death at that moment on the plateau when he caught sight of the Yeti, he was quite sure of what he had seen. And he would be forever grateful to his Sherpa guides for quite possibly saving his life.

SPRING-
HEELED
JACK

COULD terrifying monsters be hiding somewhere along the winding streets and lonely lanes of London? Werewolves, huge black dogs, and even fierce and snarling cats reportedly all lurk there, attacking those citizens of London who are unfortunate enough to be traveling its streets late at night.

Perhaps the most horrible creature of them all was known as Spring-heeled Jack, a monster who terrorized London and its suburbs in the

47

1800s. The strange monster seemed to be able to change forms at will. Sometimes he was a white bull. Other times he appeared as a bear or an enormous baboon. According to one report, he even wore a strange metallic armor.

Despite which form he chose, Spring-heeled Jack displayed one incredible talent—he could leap to great heights or over great distances. That talent allowed him to spring upon his victims quickly, before they knew what hit them. And, after he had attacked them, it allowed him to escape in seconds.

Most of those who were attacked by Spring-heeled Jack died of their wounds. Those who didn't went crazy afterwards. However, one London woman survived her encounter with the hideous creature. Her story serves as a vivid warning to others who might be fooled by a creature's evil deceptions.

A cold and bitter wind blew in London and Jane Alsop decided to skip the theater that evening. The weather was not the only reason to stay indoors. Rumors raged about a horrible creature, a creature known by the odd name of Spring-heeled Jack. Loose on the streets of

London, the creature attacked its victims suddenly, springing upon them from behind, and then scratching and beating them. Then he would disappear just as quickly, leaving them to await help—or death.

Thinking about the tales made Jane shiver. Jane had heard that just two nights ago Lucy Scales and her sister had been attacked at the entrance to Green Dragon Alley. The newspaper reported that the monster had breathed fire onto Lucy's face and had burned her mouth and lips. Both women had been taken to a hospital, where they began to have violent fits. Neither woman was able to tell authorities exactly what had happened. Both could recall only basic details.

Jane tried not to think about the stories as she sat in front of the fire at her parents' home. She knew her sisters, Mary and Sarah, were safe upstairs reading in their rooms. But Jane was older and she liked to stay up late, writing in her journal.

Suddenly, Jane heard a sound that made her jump. It was a loud and boisterous knocking at the front gate. "That's strange," Jane said aloud to herself. "It's an odd time of night for visitors."

Then she heard someone call out, "I'm a policeman. I need your help!"

Jane walked to the front door and opened it just a crack. At the gate that blocked the house from the street was a gentleman dressed as a policeman. He wore a long, black cloak with a hood, which was typical of this time period.

"Bring me a light!" the man shouted in an official-sounding voice. "We've got Spring-heeled Jack in the lane. And hurry!"

Jane shut the door and went looking for a candle. *What a relief,* she thought to herself. *Spring-heeled Jack has finally been caught. Now it will be safe to go out at night again!*

Jane lit the candle, cupped it with her hand to protect it from the wind, and headed out the door to help the policeman. She decided she would hand him the candle and let him go about his business of taking the creature away. Jane knew she didn't want to see the monster.

She got close to the gate and handed the candle through the grating to the policeman. Immediately, he flung his cloak aside. Jane gasped. He wasn't a policeman at all.

Standing directly in front of her on the other side of the gate was a strange-looking creature.

He wore a large helmet-like hat on his head. On his body, he wore a skin-tight suit of a white material. Large bloodshot eyes bulged from the eye holes in his helmet.

Before Jane could turn and run, the creature spit blue and white flames at her face. Jane could feel the heat just inches from her skin. Although the flames did not touch her face, she smelled a hideous stench of smoke and flesh.

Her heart pounding, Jane tried to scream, but she couldn't make a sound.

Then the thing poked its long, talon-like fingers through the metal grating and began tearing at her dress. Jane was desperate. She tried to run, but the thing had one of its hands grasped tightly around her arm. The other hand raked sharp claws across her face.

Jane swallowed hard and tried once again to scream. This time, a long, bloodcurdling scream came from her constricted throat.

The creature grabbed at her more furiously, trying to pull her through the gate. Blood and tears ran down Jane's face. She screamed a-gain, a scream borne of fear and pain.

Suddenly she felt hands pull her from the

other direction. Mary and Sarah pulled her away from the creature and toward the house. But the creature was stronger than they were. It pulled her closer and closer against the gate. Jane could feel the heat from its mouth.

Finally, Sarah and Mary yanked her free. They ran with her crumpled body in their arms into the house and shut the door.

Inside, they tended to Jane's wounds and hoped that she would not suffer any long-lasting emotional damage.

But Jane wasn't Spring-heeled Jack's only victim that night. The next day, the newspaper reported that just down the block the body of another woman had been found. Her face had been scratched repeatedly and her hair was singed by fire. An unnamed source said the woman had responded to a call from someone outside her house—someone who had claimed to be a policeman.

Only he wasn't a policeman. He was Spring-heeled Jack in the same disguise he had used to fool Jane Alsop.

For several years after, reports of Spring-heeled Jack's horrible attacks continued to appear in the London papers. Every time Jane read one of them, she realized how lucky she had been to escape with her life.

Then the reports suddenly stopped—as if Spring-heeled Jack had died or had gone into hiding. Nevertheless, Jane could not rest easy. She couldn't help wondering if the horrible creature was still out there, somewhere, waiting to trick its next victim into a hideous encounter—an encounter that would surely end in death.

THE DREADED TAW OF THAILAND

*C*AN *perfectly normal human beings turn into hideous, terrifying killer-creatures? History is full of stories of these kinds of transformations. Witches can supposedly transform themselves into black cats and back again. Other legends claim that people with certain evil connections can turn into giant birds or snarling dogs or even slithering snakes.*

Perhaps the most horrifying tale of all is the story of the werewolf. Human being by day, wolf by night, the werewolf is a vicious killer. In its wolf stage, it strikes without warning, biting the neck of its victim. Werewolf stories have been part of the folklore of England and Scotland for years. This story, however, comes to us from a place farther away, which proves that there's no escape from the terror of the werewolf.

Ever since Harold Young had arrived in Thailand, he had heard legends of the terrifying Taw. The natives said it was a wolf-like creature that hunted people down and then killed them by biting them in the neck. But the Taw was not a wolf all the time. Rumors indicated that the Taw was really a man—most of the time. But when evil forces overtook him, he transformed into the Taw. Then, after he had murdered a human being in his typical grisly fashion, he transformed himself back, once again, into a man.

Harold scoffed at the stories. They sounded a bit like the stories he had heard back in his homeland, England. There, a similar man/wolf creature supposedly hunted down hapless victims and, after its bloody work was finished, it also turned back into a man. The British had their own name for the creature—a werewolf. Harold considered the tale to be absolute nonsense. He didn't know how the stories got started or where they would end. He only knew that he didn't believe them.

Harold had originally come to Thailand as an ambassador, but after his post ended, he found that he couldn't leave. He loved the country—the deep green of the dark jungle, the misty gray of the night sky, and the wonderful rainbow of colors he saw in the marketplaces in the cities. Most of all, he loved to hunt the various creatures that inhabited the jungles. (It was the early 1960s, and laws protecting endangered species had not been passed yet.) Harold could hunt whatever he chose, and he was determined to bag a panther or two as a trophy for his home in London.

Harold packed up his gear and headed for the Lahu Mountains, near the Thai border. Before he left Bangkok, he was told that a Taw had been terrorizing the area, but he paid the warning no mind. *Silly nonsense,* he thought. *Just rumors spread by superstitious natives.* The Taw was nothing for him to worry about.

When he arrived at the small village that was to serve as a base for his hunting expedition, the village was abuzz with more stories of the Taw. Reportedly, it had attacked two young women in the village just to the north. In each case, it had killed the woman by tearing out her throat. When villagers followed its footsteps, they were surprised to find that the wolf-like tracks became human footprints after just a few yards.

Harold believed that the girls had been killed, but he figured it was probably just a wild animal that got them. The jungle was a cruel place, and sometimes human beings became victims of vicious animal attacks.

The hunter had no luck on his first day in the jungle. In fact, he didn't see a single species of wild game. It was eerie, almost as if the creatures had left the jungle entirely. Even the noisy birds that usually screeched from above were silent. At dusk, he headed back to the village.

He had just reached the edge of the small collection of huts when he heard a blood-curdling scream come from the shadows. He immediately dashed toward the sound.

He stopped short to stare at what was before him.

There, in the dimness, stood a wolf-like creature. It was covered with dark, matted fur. Its eyes glowed a hideous yellow in the darkness. Blood dripped from its long, sharp fangs.

But it was the look on its face that sent fear to the depth of Harold's heart. It was a look of evil pleasure, as if the creature had been thoroughly enjoying some sort of wicked task.

Then, in horror, Harold realized what that task had been. Beside the creature, a young woman lay in a bloody heap.

His hands shaking, Harold pulled his rifle around from his back. Trying to steady himself, he aimed the gun directly at the creature's yellow eyes. The creature growled fiercely and then turned away. Harold held his breath and squeezed the trigger.

The creature recoiled as if it had been hit in the left shoulder. Then it continued running toward the jungle.

The villagers had heard the gunshot and ran from their huts toward Harold and the young girl. Under the light of a torch one of them carried, Harold could see that the girl was dead. Her screams had been silenced by the creature's bloody attack. Her throat had been completely torn out.

"It is the work of the Taw!" one of the villagers cried.

"Evil one!" another one yelled.

Harold turned to the small crowd that had gathered. "It was a wolf, all right, but I don't believe there is such a creature as a Taw. It was a wolf, plain and simple. Tomorrow at sunup, I'll prove it," he said.

"But how?" one asked

"I will follow its tracks and find its lair. Then, if it is not dead already from my gunshot, I will kill it. It won't bother you again."

The villagers murmured among themselves. "But it is evil—half man, half-wolf," one said.

"I will find it," Harold answered forcefully. "Now it's best we tend to this body."

The next day dawned warm and sunny. Harold checked his ammunition and prepared for the hunt of his lifetime. He would prove once and for all that the Taw didn't exist.

The day was completely unlike the day before. The birds were screeching as they usually did. Scuffling sounds among the bushes meant that the jungle's inhabitants had returned and were startled by Harold's presence.

The footprints of the creature were easy to distinguish in the early morning light. Here and there, small pools of dried blood appeared. The creature must have bled all the way to his lair.

Just half a mile into the jungle, the tracks ended beside a huge boulder. Harold shook his head. Where could the creature have gone?

His rifle at the ready, Harold quietly and slowly made his way around the boulder.

He gasped when he saw what was on the other side. There, lying at his feet face-down, was a man.

There was a brown circle of blood on the jungle floor just in front of the man. Harold looked closer at him. Perhaps he, too, had been the victim of some wild animal attack. Harold checked for signs of life. There were none.

But the man appeared to be unharmed.

Then Harold saw it—a round bullet hole in the man's shoulder. The bullet hole was in the exact spot where he had shot the creature—the creature that the villagers called the Taw. There could be no other explanation. The legend of the Taw was true. The creature had bled its victim and then transformed back into its human form. But the wound Harold had inflicted while the creature was in his wolf form was too much for him to survive.

Harold had indeed bagged the prey of his lifetime, but this one would not end up on his trophy wall. Harold would simply have to live with the memory. He was only glad to have rid this part of the world of an evil and hideous creature.

MEETING AT LOCH NESS

*T*HE *dark waters of the Scottish lake known as Loch Ness look peaceful enough, but local folks warn of terrible danger there. They say the lake is the home of a terrible creature, a huge swimming monster. A dinosaur-like creature was supposedly seen in the lake as early as 565 A.D. by Columba, an Irish saint. Since that time, the monster has been sighted in the lake thousands of times. Usually, it is just the head that is seen above the lake's surface.*

Occasionally, though, the monster treats tourists to a full view of the giant humps that appear to be on his back.

Is the monster fact or fiction? Could the same monster live for thousands of years in the lake? Or have there been subsequent generations of the monster known as Nessie? Perhaps there are entire families of these monsters. If that is true, why haven't they been seen more often? And why haven't the scientists who have searched the lake's waters come up with any sign of the monster's existence?

These are questions that people have been asking for centuries. One man answered one of the questions: He discovered that the monster was real. And because of his encounter, he had the snapshot to prove it.

Colonel Wilson had really enjoyed his trip to the Scottish Highlands. The land was a bit wild to the north and it was rich in wild game. Wilson didn't hunt game with a rifle or bow and arrow, though. He hunted with his camera. A surgeon by trade, Wilson was an amateur nature photographer and he had gotten some of his best shots on this trip.

Along the many large lakes that dotted the countryside, various kinds of water birds gathered, some of which he had never seen in his hometown of London. And the weather had been fabulous—the lighting just perfect.

On the last day of his trip, Wilson convinced his buddy to take an early morning drive along the north shore of the lake known as Loch Ness. The lake had become famous in Scottish history for the legends of the huge monster that was said to live beneath its waters. But Wilson didn't really believe the stories he had heard. How could a monster live for so many years in the lake and never be captured?

When Wilson saw the size of the lake, he had to admit that it could be possible. He had thought the lake would be as small as a pond, but the expanse before him was huge. Sharp cliffs lined either side of the lake and then dropped sharply down into the water. The water itself was a dark, inky black.

"Polluted water?" he asked his friend as the car pulled into an overlook. "How could it be? There are no factories up this way."

"It's from the peat," his friend answered. "The water runs through peat moss before it reaches the lake. It picks up small particles of peat, and that's what turns the water black."

"Hmmm," Wilson answered. "Looks deep."

"I've heard that there are places more than nine hundred feet deep. There are supposed to be caves all along the sides, underneath the water. Don't know if that's true, or if it's just what folks say to support the whole idea of the monster. You know, they might claim the monster could hide in those caves," Wilson's friend said.

Wilson just shook his head and chuckled. Crazy business, this Loch Ness monster rumor. How could people believe such things?

Wilson attached a telephoto lens to his camera and aimed it at the lake. Through his lens, he could see the lake's smooth surface, not broken by even so much as a ripple. Then he aimed it at the sky where some birds were circling. Other than that slight movement, the morning was quiet—eerily quiet.

Wilson focused his camera back on the lake.

Suddenly the water rippled, just slightly. "Must be some fish in there," Wilson said to his friend.

"Yeah," he answered. "Too bad we forgot our poles."

Wilson laughed. From their position on the cliff, there was no way they could get close enough to the water to fish.

Suddenly, Wilson heard his friend gasp.

Wilson quickly aimed his camera at the spot where his friend was pointing. A section of the water was churning. Dark foam formed on its surface.

Then, as Wilson watched through his camera, the neck and head of some long, dark creature became visible above the inky water. The thing slowly stretched upward, as if testing the air. The neck was narrow and graceful. The head was long and triangular shaped. It almost looked like some kind of dinosaur—a brontosaurus, perhaps. Through his camera, Wilson could see that its skin was a deep, dark green.

Wilson's first impulse was to run for the car. What if the monster came after them? Then he realized that that was just a bit unlikely. The monster had never been known to leave its watery home and, even if it did, it probably couldn't reach them on the side of the cliff. Instead, Wilson wasted no time recording the scene with his camera. He had only four pictures left on his roll, but he snapped them quickly in succession. Then, as he was reaching for his extra film, the huge green creature slowly and quietly slid beneath the black surface of Loch Ness. The water churned for just a few seconds. And then the lake became calm again.

His friend was still rubbing his eyes in disbelief. "Could it be? Did we really see it?" he sputtered.

Wilson shook his head. "I don't know what we saw. Maybe it was just the morning light playing tricks on us."

"But it sure looked . . ."

"Real? Wilson finished. "I got some snapshots of it. That will tell us for sure."

The two hopped into their car and raced into Inverness. They stopped at the first pharmacy they could find that was open at that hour of the morning and left the film. Then the two headed off to breakfast, still speculating about what they had seen.

Several of the townsfolk overheard their conversation and crowded around their table.

"You really saw Nessie?" one asked.

"I heard tell of her, but never saw her," said another.

"My boy, he says he's seen that monster, but I didn't believe him."

It seemed everyone had an opinion about the lake monster, and they weren't shy about sharing it. Wilson and his friend could barely get away from the crowd when it was time to pick up the photos.

They finally managed to leave the group and then headed for the pharmacy. There, Wilson's hand trembled as he opened the photographs.

The first shots were of some quail he had seen earlier in the week. Those were followed by a picture of a red deer in the evening light and some shots of unusual butterflies he had seen in a meadow. Then, finally, came the pictures he had been waiting for.

Wilson gazed at the first picture he had taken of the lake. It only showed the broad expanse of dark water. No creature. He sighed and flipped to the next photo. Just the inky black lake. There was nothing to indicate that any living creature was there.

The next shot was completely black, somehow overexposed in the developing process.

Finally, he turned to the last picture. Wilson gasped. There it was—a real picture of the monster of Loch Ness. Its long neck was visible, floating gracefully above the water. And its head appeared as a gentle triangle against the sky, about twelve feet above the water's surface.

Wilson's picture caused a rage that, within a few years, spread through Scotland and the rest of the world. Finally, there was proof of the monster's existence. Though some claimed the photo had been doctored or was the work of trick photography, Wilson knew it was neither. From that moment, scientists began searching for the monster that Wilson had photographed.

Even so, though many have reported seeing Nessie and a few have even taken some photographs, no one has discovered anything else about this mysterious creature of the deep.

THE
EVIL
OF THE
WHITE
TIGER

A tiger pacing back and forth behind the bars of a cage at a zoo is scary enough. Meeting a tiger in its natural habitat, uncaged, is far more frightening. But this kind of encounter is very unlikely to happen. Most tigers steer clear of human beings. In fact, tigers have more to fear from human beings who often hunt and kill them than humans have to fear from tigers.

To the natives of India, though, tigers are far more than just ferocious cats. Indians believe *that tigers have special supernatural power. And they often perceive the tiger's power to be an evil force that is turned against human beings.*

In the early 1900s one British officer learned just how powerful this evil was. It was a bloody and tragic lesson.

When Colonel DeSilva heard the story of a man-eating tiger threatening the Indian village where he lived, he said one word—"Hogwash!"

DeSilva had been hearing rumors of these giant, blood-thirsty beasts for as long as he had been in India, but he had never really heard of anyone actually being attacked. He knew enough about the wild to know that tigers avoided human beings altogether. Oh, occasionally a sick or old tiger, too old to catch its prey, would wander into a village and attack a dog, but DeSilva had never read a reputable account of a tiger attacking people.

This new rumor was the weirdest and most improbable one he had ever heard. Natives said that a huge, white tiger with icy blue eyes was threatening the people of India and that this ferocious man-eater was a killing machine whose hunger could not be satisfied. According to one story, the creature had wiped out an entire village, eating its inhabitants one by one. Another story claimed that the tiger was particularly fond of eating children and that it had robbed one town of all of its youngsters.

But the attacks were never proven. And no attacks had ever occurred in DeSilva's village. DeSilva believed that the entire tale was nothing but supernatural nonsense. He knew that the Indians had a strong belief about tigers— that the tigers had some supernatural power and that they were motivated by some evil force. They claimed that when a tiger attacked a village, it was punishing the village people for some horrible wrongdoing.

Besides a worse enemy than a pale, white tiger was lurking among the Indians. It was a disease called leprosy and it ended in a horrible, shameful death. The disease actually ate away at human skin until nothing was left. As it devoured the body, the disease caused horrifying disfigurement. At times, actual body parts seemed to fall off completely.

Because leprosy was considered to be extremely contagious and because of the gruesome

way it made people look, people with leprosy—
lepers—were often shunned by their family and
their communities.

One day DeSilva discovered that leprosy
had struck the small village where he lived.

One of the elders of the village was dying—
in the last stages of the disease. Although he
knew he was about to see a horrible sight,
DeSilva decided to visit the man in order to pay
his last respects. That was the proper thing to
do, and DeSilva was always proper.

Colonel DeSilva swallowed hard as he en-
tered the small hut where the man lay dying.
He had seen the hideous effects of leprosy
before, but he still wasn't prepared for what he
saw in front of him. The man's face was almost
raw. Pieces of dead skin hung from his ears
and nose.

The man moaned when he saw DeSilva.
Then he tried to speak. The words came out in
a sort of half croak. "Tiger-r-r . . .," the man
said. "White tiger."

DeSilva shook his head. "There's no tiger
here, old chap. Come now, you mustn't worry
about it. The whole thing is just a lot of crazy
nonsense."

The man shook his head back and forth. "No!" he insisted, as loudly as he could manage. "You must save me from it."

"There's no tiger," DeSilva replied. "You must be delirious."

"It will come," the man insisted. "You must save me."

DeSilva had had enough of this nonsense. He had come to pay his respects, not to discuss some fictional beast. He turned to leave.

But DeSilva suddenly stopped when he saw what was in front of him. His blood seemed to freeze in terror.

Blocking the doorway to the outside was a huge, pale tiger. Its ice-blue eyes glowed fiercely. Its lips were pulled back and its huge, sharp teeth shone brightly. It growled a low and threatening growl.

"You must save me!" the old man shouted from his bed.

The tiger sniffed the air as if deciding which to eat first. DeSilva stood frozen to the spot. Although many others had taken to carrying a gun with them at all times to fight off attacks, DeSilva hadn't brought one. After all, he didn't believe in the phantom tiger in the first place.

The tiger crouched low, preparing to pounce. DeSilva's breath came in fast gasps. The sound of blood rushed in his ears.

From his makeshift bed on the floor, the old man moaned. Then he cried, "Save me or be forever cursed."

The tiger growled again. DeSilva looked from the old man to the tiger and back again. Then he watched in horror as the tiger sprung into the air.

The tiger went directly for the old leper.

The old man let out a horrible, piercing scream. DeSilva saw his chance and headed out the door of the hut, determined to get help. As he ran away, he heard the man scream one more time and then yell, "A curse on you!"

Then he heard nothing more. DeSilva summoned his fellow soldiers, but he knew it would be too late.

By the time they got to the hut, the old man was gone. The tiger had attacked its prey and then had taken it into the jungle to eat it more slowly.

The episode haunted DeSilva. If only he had believed the rumors, he would have brought a gun with him. He could have saved the old man. His wife tried to comfort him, but it didn't really help. He felt completely responsible for the entire bloody incident.

A year passed and DeSilva somehow managed to live with the memory, allowing it to slip to the back of his mind most of the time. But the rumors started again.

The ghostly white tiger had come back, the Indians reported, and once again it was going about its bloody business. This time, DeSilva took the rumors seriously and kept a gun with him at all times. If the tiger appeared, he would kill it once and for all. Its reign of terror would finally be over.

One evening, just as the sun was setting, DeSilva had his chance. He, his wife, and their two-year-old son were sitting on the lawn of their large estate, enjoying the cool weather.

DeSilva heard the low growl, first from the bushes beside the house. The scene from that fateful day in the leper's hut flashed in his mind. The terror he had felt then turned to rage. He wanted to shoot the beast and watch as it bled to death.

The growl came again. DeSilva reached for his gun and whispered for his wife to take their son into the house.

But the tiger was swift and clever. Before DeSilva could even cock his gun, it pounced. DeSilva's wife released a bloodcurdling scream. DeSilva gasped as he saw where the tiger lunged. It headed directly at his son.

DeSilva shouldered his gun, aimed, and fired. The white beast fell to the ground in a heap. DeSilva ran toward his son and his wife.

When he saw their faces, still drawn in terror, he sighed deeply. They had survived. His son had a long scratch on his cheek where the tiger had clawed at him, but he was safe. DeSilva had killed the tiger once and for all.

He looked in the direction of the beast. He wanted to take a hard look at this horrible creature before calling the authorities.

But the tiger was gone—as if it had disappeared in mid-air. Neither DeSilva nor his wife had seen it get up and leave—which would have been unlikely at any rate, given the bullet that DeSilva was sure it had lodged in its head.

But as weird as it seemed, it was gone, as if whisked away by some unseen force. DeSilva didn't wait around to investigate. He swept up his small son, put his arm around his wife's shoulders, and ushered them protectively into the house.

The tiger was never seen again in India. The forces that spirited it away had done so for good. The Indian people were grateful to De-Silva and praised his skill and his luck.

But DeSilva turned out to be not so lucky. The claw mark on his little son's face became infected. A short time after, the young boy developed a horrible case of leprosy and died a quick, but painful death.

And, no matter how hard he tried to explain it away, DeSilva feared that the old man's curse had somehow come full-circle. For failing to save the old man from the dreaded white tiger, DeSilva lost his very own son.

AN ENCOUNTER WITH BIG FOOT

*H*UNTERS *have told stories of ape-like creatures that live solitary lives in the wilderness. The creatures are shy and they rarely emerge from their remote lairs, especially when human beings are around. However, some humans beings have actually come face to face with these Bigfoot creatures. And many of these meetings have ended in absolute terror.*

Could such creatures really live in wilderness areas and yet remain almost completely undetected? What kind of creatures are they? Are they products of mutations or are they survivors of an almost-extinct species? We may never know. We do know that throughout history Bigfoot creatures have been sighted all over the North American continent. While many people have thought that Bigfoot sightings are nothing more than products of overactive imaginations, it would be hard to explain why there have been so many sightings in so many different places. In the 1920s, three men discovered something new about these huge and mysterious creatures: When one of their kind is harmed, the Bigfoots seek revenge. And their revenge is more terrifying than the creatures themselves.

Fred Beck and his fellow trappers were tired—dead tired. They had been trapping all day about seventy-five miles north of Portland in a small canyon in the Mount Saint Helens area of Washington. Trapping was hard work, but it was a living. There weren't many jobs available in the northwestern part of the United States during the 1920s. So Fred and his trapping buddies spent most of the fall and winter in a small cabin out in the wilderness. It was rough being away from his family, but Fred liked living for a season among the tall, willowy pine trees. It gave him a sense of just how incredible the natural world was.

"Time to go, Fred?" asked Allan Phillips, one of the trappers.

"Yep, I expect so. Getting near sundown." Fred looked up at the trees surrounding him and noted how the sun's rays were now slanted through the delicate pine needles. The shadows made a kind of patchwork design on the forest floor.

Then Fred saw something else through the trees—something that made his heart race in terror.

Just beyond the grove of trees was a small clearing. And standing in the middle of the clearing was some kind of huge, hairy creature. It looked like a bear—no, an ape—only it was much larger than any apes he had seen pictures of. And the creature's brown fur was long and matted in places.

Fred closed his eyes and rubbed them. He figured he was seeing things—the fading light and his own fatigue were playing tricks on him.

When he opened his eyes, the creature was still there—only now it had raised its arm above its head in a threatening motion. And its mouth was pulled back in a harsh snarl.

Fred looked over at Allan. Allan's eyes were big with terror. It seemed as if he was frozen in place, frozen by fear.

Fred slowly reached for his rifle, but the creature was no longer moving slowly. It charged toward the two men, crashing through the forest. Fred didn't wait but a second. He aimed his rifle and fired.

The creature stopped in its tracks, just a few yards in front of them. Fred thought he might have grazed its head, but he couldn't tell for sure.

He could see the creature clearly. In the split second that the creature stood in front of him, Fred tried to memorize it in detail. It was huge—maybe as tall as nine feet. Its eyes glowed a blood red. To make matters worse, its body gave off a horrible stench, a smell so powerful that Fred's eyes teared up and his throat narrowed into a gag.

Then, as if it suddenly realized that it had been shot, it turned and ran back into the woods.

Fred breathed a sigh of relief. He looked over at Allan. Allan's teeth were chattering with fear.

"W-w-w-what was that?" Allan asked.

"I don't know," Fred answered. "I've never seen anything like it. All I know is that we'd best get back to the cabin before it comes back."

The two trappers ran back to the cabin, often looking over their shoulders to make sure that the creature wasn't going to make another appearance.

That night, around a roaring fire, they told their friend, Sam Kramer, about the encounter. Sam had been trapping in another part of the woods that day. Always a skeptic, he scoffed at the two.

"You can't tell me some hairy ape has been living here all this time and we haven't once seen it. After all, we've been hunting these woods for years," Sam said.

"I'm telling you, it happened," Fred answered. "Allan here saw the thing, too."

"It was gruesome," Allan answered. "And the smell—it was enough to make you throw up."

"Come on, you two. Maybe you've been out

here in the wilderness too long. Maybe you should head back to Portland and get yourself a city job," said Sam.

Just as Sam finished his sentence, there was a loud thud against the cabin wall.

"What the—" Sam began, as he reached for his rifle.

Another thud followed, this one louder than the first. The cabin's walls trembled just a bit.

Then the thuds began in rapid succession, one after another. "It sounds like someone's throwing rocks at us. Who could it be?" Allan said, his voice weak.

"I don't know," Sam answered, "but I aim to find out."

Rifle in hand, Sam strode to the door of the cabin. Fred stayed where he was. This day had been weird enough—and now the night was turning even weirder. Whatever it was, Fred wanted to sit and wait for it to go away.

Slowly, Sam opened the door and stuck his head outside. As he did, a boulder-sized rock—too heavy for any man to lift, let alone throw—catapulted through the door.

Sam slammed the door shut.

His face was pure white.

"Looks like I owe you fellas an apology," Sam said, his voice shaking just a little. "Those ape creatures—they're real all right. And they're mad. There's a bunch of them—just at the edge of the clearing. And they're tossing boulders at us."

"W-w-w-what should we do?" Allan asked.

"I don't rightly know, " Sam answered. "We could grab our guns and fire at 'em through the door."

Bang! Another boulder hit the wall.

"I vote we stay here," Fred said. "We just stay put. They'll leave soon enough. They can't keep this up all night."

"You're right. We should try and wait it out as best we can," answered Sam.

So the three sat, huddled inside the cabin, while the rocks were hurled at them from outside. They weren't prepared for how long they would have to wait.

All night long, the creatures kept up the rock throwing, hurling one rock after another at the small cabin. Its walls held firm though, and just as the sun began spreading fingers of light against the sky, the pounding stopped.

The three still sat, huddled together, as if

not quite believing that their attackers had left.

Sam volunteered to open the door.

"But what if they are right outside, waiting to attack?"

"They could be," Sam answered, "but they could have gotten us long before now. They could have knocked down the door and killed us if they wanted to, but they didn't, did they?"

Fred couldn't argue with his logic. The three men grabbed their rifles and slowly opened the door.

The cabin was surrounded by rocks, boulders, tree limbs, and other debris. It seemed as if the creatures simply threw whatever they could get their hands on.

Among the debris were huge footprints in the dusty dirt. Fred gasped as he realized just how big the footprints were—maybe two feet long.

The creatures themselves were nowhere to be found.

It didn't take the three trappers long to make the decision to leave the woods—and quickly, before the creatures decided to come back. The men packed up their meager belongings and, rifles at the ready, they headed out of

the woods on foot toward civilization.
It was time to get city jobs.

THE
PHANTOM
SON

*C*AN a person be in two places at one time? It sounds impossible, and yet there are many well-documented cases of this happening. They seem to occur at a critical point in time, such as when a person is threatened or faces death. These reports indicate that a person can actually project himself to another place. Such appearances are known as "crisis phantoms" or "crisis apparitions." They occur most often when a person is separated from his family and loved *ones. When the crisis or disaster occurs, he is somehow able to "wish himself" away to join the ones he loves.*

Such was the case with a young man named Joseph Collyer. His love for his mother and his family must have been strong—strong enough to transport him over one thousand miles.

Anne Collyer was a worry wart. She worried about everything from her health to the weather. But mostly she worried about her family. Anne constantly worried about her five children—where they were, what they were doing, and whether they were safe.

When her son Joseph told her that he was leaving home, Anne's heart froze. Of course, she realized, that he was more than old enough to live elsewhere, but she hated to let him out of her sight. She was sure that something terrible would happen to him if he left the safe haven of his family's house.

When Joseph told her where he was going and what he planned to do, Anne worried even more. He said he was leaving to take command of a riverboat on the Mississippi. In the mid-1800s, the Mississippi River promised two things to those who were willing to navigate its muddy waters: easy passage to the Gulf of Mexico and untold adventure. Dreams of navigating the mighty river sent many young men's hearts racing.

Anne tried and tried to talk Joseph into staying in New Jersey and finding a local job, but he was determined to head west. He wanted to be a riverboat captain and that was that. On the day Joseph left his mother, his father, and his four sisters, Anne felt as if she were being ripped in two.

He regularly wrote home, but it often took months for his letters to travel the one thousand miles to reach his family. Anne loved his letters, but they only made her worry even more about him. It was rough country out there and seemed to her to be very dangerous. Soon Anne's worrying grew until she was terrified, and she knew she would remain that way until she saw her son again.

And Anne was going to see him sooner than she realized.

January 12th was a bitterly cold day. All day long, the wind howled outside their house, flinging icy snow against the windows. The storm made it difficult to get the girls to sleep that night. After settling them in, Anne herself went to bed early, saying a prayer for her son as she got ready. Her husband stayed down-stairs, tending the fire.

Just as Anne bent over to snuff out the candle, she saw an incredible sight—right there in her room.

Joseph! He was home! But he was hurt—hurt badly.

Joseph's head was covered with bloody bandages. A stream of blood trickled from his hairline to his chin. Large purplish bruises covered his face and neck. One eye was swollen completely shut. His arm hung limply in a sling.

How did he get home? What happened to him? Whatever it was, Anne knew he had to be in horrible pain.

But, strangely enough, he didn't look as if he was suffering. He didn't speak, but only smiled a slow, peaceful smile. His eyes shone in the darkness, and they held a gentle, kind expression.

"Joseph!" she cried, stretching out her arms to embrace him. Her son looked at her with a deep, serene stare. Then, slowly and deliberately, he turned and walked away. As he reached her bedroom door, his image faded. Then, without a word, Joseph disappeared.

Anne ran down the stairs, her heart pounding. She didn't know what the image of Joseph meant, but she knew that he was in trouble of some kind—terrible trouble. She had to tell her husband.

Anne's husband was a reasonable man and he knew his wife well. She always expected the worst when it came to her children, and he was sure that tonight her worries about Joseph had simply turned into a nightmare.

"A dream," he said from his armchair by the fire. "It was only a dream." He took his wife in his arms and stroked her hair. "You worry too much about Joseph. It's no wonder that you had a nightmare about him being hurt."

But the words did little to comfort her. She was overcome with a feeling of dread. She wept most of the night, thinking about her son in bandages, bleeding from an open wound. She knew that she would not rest again until she received some word about him, some sign that he was all right.

Two weeks later, Anne got the news. An official-looking letter arrived from the steamship line her son worked for. Her hands trembled as she opened it.

The letter expressed condolences to the Collyer family on behalf of the steamship company. It explained that her son had been killed in a horrible accident. His steamship had collided with another. Part of the ship's mast had fallen on Joseph's face and neck. He had tried to cushion his fall with his arm and broke it in the process. The note said that he had lived for three days following the accident. The letter went on to report that just before his death, Joseph seemed to be completely free of pain. He died peacefully that late January night.

Anne's blood ran cold as she finished the rest of the letter. Joseph had died at exactly 10:30 on the night of January 12th—the precise time and day she had seen her son in her bedroom, his head wrapped in bandages, his face bruised, his arm broken.

But then Anne remembered the look she had seen on Joseph's face. It was the peaceful look of acceptance. This memory comforted Anne most as she grieved the loss of her son.

Joseph's love for his mother had been so strong that he crossed many barriers to tell her goodbye. He crossed miles and even time. But most of all, he crossed the barrier between this world and the next in order to leave his mother with one parting gift—the peace of knowing he was at rest.

THE
MOTH
MONSTER

*T*HEY *are large, birdlike creatures with glowing red eyes. Their wings are huge, spanning at least twelve feet. They are not covered with feathers, but with dull, gray skin. And as hideous as they look, what they do is far worse. They have been known to swoop down upon unsuspecting human beings, carrying them off in their sharp claws. And what they do with the human beings they catch, no one really knows.*

It sounds like something out of a weird science fiction movie, but these creatures are real—terrifyingly real. History is full of reports of these flying beasts, and the accounts have come from all over the world. The monsters have been seen in the skies over Russia, England, Vietnam, Brazil, and the United States.

Are these creatures left over from the dinosaur age? Are they some sort of strange mutation, half-human and half-bird? Or are they aliens visiting our planet from a different world? No one knows for sure, but we do know that to encounter them is to experience terror. And, as a father and daughter discovered one night on a lonely road in West Virginia, such an encounter can even be deadly.

Sally Andrews hadn't really wanted to go out on that misty night in September, but her father had convinced her to. It was a perfect night for hunting, he said, and they needed food for the family table.

Sally actually kind of enjoyed these early evening hunting trips with her dad. Just after sunset when the moon was low in the sky, the critters in the woods around her Point Pleasant home came out of hiding. Possum, rabbits, groundhogs, and raccoons all scurried around in the underbrush.

The father and daughter had decided to head to Cornstalk Hunting Grounds. They usually had good luck there. Even though the grounds were just off the major highway, they were always plentiful with small game.

The two talked and laughed as they rode along. Sally's dad was always quick with a joke, and he told a few as he guided the car along the dark roadway.

Suddenly, he slammed on the brakes. Sally's seat belt pulled taut against her shoulders.

Ahead of them, in the beam of the head-lights, Sally could see a strange figure. It looked like a man, but it was much larger. A giant almost. Sally looked over at her father. Sweat beaded on his brow. His eyes were wide in terror.

Sally closed her eyes, sure she was imagin-ing things. But when she opened them again, the huge thing was still there, just standing in the middle of the road. The moon came out from behind a cloud and Sally could see it more clearly. It didn't seem to have a head of any kind. And there were two gray humps, one on either side.

"Daddy?" Sally said, her voice shaking.

Her father didn't answer. He turned and looked at her, his face ghostly white.

Suddenly, two bright red lights seemed to turn on from the top of the creature's body where its eyes would have been. The lights glowed blood-red in the darkness. Sally was so terrified that she would do anything to get away. Why didn't her father just back the car away and get them out of there? She looked over at him. He was frozen with fear, completely unable to move.

Sally reached across him and pushed hard on the car's horn. A long honk sounded in the night.

As if responding to the honk, the creature turned around quickly. Then the two gray humps unfolded. Now Sally could see what they were. They were wide wings, lined with deep red veins. And they were as wide as the road itself.

But as wide and horrible as they looked, the blood-striped wings weren't the most terrifying feature of the flying beast. Beneath the wings, hung two claws. On the claws were silver points, flashing in the darkness. The claws were extended in Sally's direction, as if they threatened to carry her away.

The creature took to the air, its shining talons extended, its giant wings making a deafening flapping sound as it hovered over their car. Then it disappeared into the gray clouds.

Sally's breath caught in her throat. Then a fierce shivering took over her body. She looked over at her dad. The color was returning to his face, but the look of terror remained. It was a look Sally had never seen before.

Then her dad stepped on the gas with such force that Sally's body was flung against the seat. Her seat belt dug into her skin as the car zoomed away.

It wasn't until they were safely back in town that Sally's dad stopped the car.

He gave Sally a long, sad look. "I didn't think it would ever come back," he said, slowly shaking his head.

"Come back? What do you mean, Dad? What was that thing?" asked Sally.

Sally's dad sighed. "I'm not sure what it is,

honey. The old timers call it the Mothman and they say it used to be seen around these parts all the time. But the stories were just jokes, used to scare little kids at night, you know."

Sally's dad stopped suddenly, a faraway look in his eyes.

"Have you ever seen it before, Daddy?" Sally asked.

"Once," he said. "When I was about your age. I was out hunting with my uncle and it swooped down from the sky like some huge, ugly bat. My uncle had his gun at his side and he fired at it twice. I was sure that he hit it, but it didn't seem to be wounded—like the bullets couldn't touch it." He paused for a moment, shaking slightly.

"And then it happened," he continued. "The thing swooped down and grabbed my uncle in its claws."

His voice choked on a sob. Sally could see his eyes filling with tears.

"It carried him off, just a little ways, then it dropped him. I can still hear him screaming as he fell to the ground and then rolled over the edge of a cliff."

"Did he . . ."

"Die?" Sally's father finished for her. "Yes, he did. And I never told a soul how it happened. I didn't think anyone would believe me. So I said he lost his balance and fell off the cliff. I told the story that way so many times, I began to believe it. I began to think that the Mothman was some crazy dream or a hallucination. Until tonight. Now I know the truth. The Mothman is real."

Sally shook her head as she listened to her father's story. Now she knew the truth, too. And she also knew something else. She and her father had been lucky. They had survived their encounter with the horrible Mothman. She shuddered as she thought about how easily they could have become the Mothman's next victims.

ALIEN NIGHT

HAS Earth ever been visited by creatures from another world? Many people think that aliens frequently visit us. Some individuals even claim to have come face to face with alien life forms, known as an encounter of the third kind. A few people tell stories of actually being abducted by alien creatures. Sometimes they have reported that the aliens performed strange tests on them, as if the aliens were trying to learn more about our species.

Remarkably, most alien stories have striking similarities. Reports routinely state that the aliens arrive in a round, metallic craft, and that their arrival and departure almost always cause some sort of electro-magnetic disturbance in the atmosphere. Descriptions of the creatures themselves are remarkably similar, as well. They reportedly are short, have large heads, have no noses or mouths, and have slits for eyes. They also seem to exert some sort of mind control over the humans they encounter, sometimes completely paralyzing them.

Many people are skeptical of alien encounters, but the encounters happen so frequently that they are difficult to explain away.

One night in Mississippi, two friends out for a night of fishing experienced something otherworldly. In the end, one of them had no doubt that he had come face to face with creatures from beyond our own solar system. He also had no doubt that he and his friend were lucky to have escaped with their lives.

The night was clear and cool when Sam Johnson and Ted Jasper headed to the pier along the Pascagoula River for a couple of hours of fishing. It had been hot and muggy all day, too hot for the fish to bite, but the cool night air would wake them up again. Sam hoped to bag a couple of catfish for dinner and Ted was sure this would be the night he'd finally pull a small-mouth bass from the river's waters.

They had been fishing from the pier right next to the shipyard for about an hour with no luck.

"How about we try some different bait?" Ted asked his friend, reaching for the tackle box.

Sam agreed and began to wind in his line. Suddenly, a strange zipping sound broke through the night air. Sam and Ted looked toward the riverbank where the noise had come from. Neither of them could believe what they saw.

There, hovering over the river's edge, was a long, silver craft. Underneath it, an eerie blue light flashed. Sam's heart began to pound in fear. His first instinct was to run away from the huge machine, but he seemed unable to move. It was as if he was paralyzed, somehow stuck on the corner of the pier.

What Sam saw next was even more terrifying. Although there was no door on the craft, it seemed simply to open up. Three pale, white creatures floated just beyond the craft. Sam noticed that they were about five feet tall and that their skin was a gray-white color. They had no hands, but instead had what looked like claws or pincers at the ends of their long arms. They had no eyes at all, but Sam could tell that they knew exactly where he and his friend were. They were coming directly at them through the night sky.

Sam tried to scream, but his voice seemed to be as paralyzed as his body. He tried to pull his eyes away from the creatures, but couldn't move his head or close his eyelids. He was forced to stare directly into their hollow, eyeless faces. Even in his terror, he noticed their other weird features—two ears shaped like cones and a large, gaping hole where their mouths should have been.

The three creatures stopped right in front of the boys and floated in the cool night air. Suddenly, Sam heard a buzzing sound, and before he knew what was happening, he was floating in the air right beside them. Although he felt nothing, he was somehow being pulled above the pier where his fishing gear lay. To his horror, Sam suddenly realized where he was going—toward the silver craft. He couldn't turn his head to look back to see what was happening to Ted, but he hoped he was somehow being spared, that he was left behind by the strange creatures.

The rest of the encounter progressed like some horrible nightmare. The creatures took Sam to a room that was lit bright yellow, although he saw no light fixtures anywhere. While Sam was still floating in midair, one of the creatures pulled his body out straight, causing him to lie down. Again Sam tried to move, but his entire body was paralyzed. Only his eyes could move and they took in every terrifying detail.

Sam watched helplessly as one of the creatures used a strange metal instrument that looked like some sort of large camera. The creature moved it back and forth across Sam's body. He felt nothing as the instrument passed over him. Then the creatures turned him on his side and did the same thing. It was as if the instrument was examining every inch of his skin, every part of his body.

The creatures themselves moved slowly but

efficiently. Their movements seemed automatic somehow, as if they were robots with a task to complete. They didn't try to communicate in any way with Sam. Instead, they seemed to be unconcerned that he was human, that he had feelings, or that he could communicate. He was treated like a laboratory animal, a specimen to be analyzed.

After what seemed to be hours, the strange examination came to an end. One of the creatures tugged at Sam with its scissor-like hands. Sam began to float in midair again, back down toward the pier. Ahead of him, he saw his friend Ted slumped as if he was sleeping at the edge of the dock.

When he reached the pier, Sam discovered he was able to move again on his own. He tried to stand up as the creatures floated away in the distance, but he couldn't. His knees were weak and his arms were trembling. He fell to his knees on the pier's rough wooden slats. Ted lay on the dock beside him, his face white and pasty, his eyes closed. With shaky hands, Sam reached over and touched his friend. Ted's eyes slowly opened.

"I-I must have fallen asleep," Ted responded,

smiling and unaware that anything strange had happened.

"You don't remember?" Sam asked in disbelief. "You don't know what went on?"

Ted looked blankly at his friend. "I don't know what you're talking about," he answered, his voice slow and hoarse as if he was just waking up. "We were fishing and we fell asleep. I guess nothing's biting."

Sam decided not to try to explain it to his friend. He doubted that Ted would believe him anyway. Instead, he gathered his gear, and the two headed to the car. Sam spent the rest of the night trying to convince himself that it hadn't happened, that it had been just some strange dream.

When the sun rose, Sam still hadn't talked himself out of the incident. No matter how crazy it sounded, he had to report it to someone. He headed straight to the sheriff's office and gave his report.

Sam was surprised by how carefully the officer listened to his story. Sam had been sure that the authorities would laugh at him or call him crazy. But this officer was taking notes, recording the smallest details.

After Sam was finished, the officer scratched his head. "Strange," he said. "This is the third report of a UFO I've taken this morning. Either the whole town is going crazy or we've just had a bunch of close encounters right here in Mississippi."

Sam swallowed hard. Others had seen the craft, too. Had they been taken aboard as he had? He would find out, he vowed to himself. He would track down the others and see if they had experienced the same weird examination.

Sam never went fishing again on that lonely pier on the Pascagoula River and he spent the next few years trying to make sense of what had happened. He underwent hypnosis and took a lie detector test. Under hypnosis he gave a vivid description of what had happened. The lie detector test reported that he was absolutely telling the truth.

He eventually found and talked with others who claimed to have had similar experiences. They all reported the same thing—the inability to move, the strange eyeless creatures with the gaping mouths, the weird examinations. It gave Sam a strange sense of comfort—a comfort mixed with terror.

Eventually, he had to face the truth about what happened. He had been a guinea pig in some strange alien experiment. He only hoped that the creatures wouldn't return to collect more data.

AN
ENCOUNTER
WITH
HISTORY

IS it possible to travel through time and visit an entirely different era? Reports of "time-slips," episodes in which people have suddenly found themselves in a different period of history, have circulated for years. Some people claim that these time-slips are proof of reincarnation, evidence that perhaps the person lived during that era in a previous life. Others claim that Earth actually has mysterious time warps that can transport people backward and forward in *time and space. Still others believe the whole concept is simply the result of an overactive imagination.*

But for two teachers visiting France, the phenomenon was all too real. And, although the two never identified what caused them to slip through time, they never had any doubts that they had actually traveled back in history.

Anne Moberly and her friend Eleanor Jourdain were excited about their trip to France. They were both French teachers and had been there before, but this time they were going to spend an entire month in romantic Paris. They planned to visit all of the historical sites they could, particularly the grand palaces and homes built during Marie Antoinette's time, just before the French Revolution. Each of them found that period of French history fascinating. It was a time when French fashions and society were at their opulent best. Of course, the era of rich lifestyles eventually brought about the downfall of France—and the beheading of Marie and her husband Louis XVI. But those events did nothing to diminish the wonder of the era, at least not as far as

Anne was concerned.

The teachers spent the first day of their trip unpacking and planning how they would spend the rest of their time there. They planned to spend the next day at Versailles, the magnificent palace built by Louis XIV, a palace that still housed some of the art world's most priceless treasures. From there, they would visit Petit Trianon, Marie Antoinette's summer home.

Anne and Eleanor headed out the next day and tried to visit Versailles, only to discover that the grand palace was closed for the day. Not to worry, Eleanor told her friend. They could head straight for Petit Trianon. They didn't have their guidebook with them, but Anne was certain she could find her way. The ladies began their journey down a narrow dirt lane that seemed familiar to them both.

Before long, though, Anne realized that she was a bit turned around. She admitted as much to Eleanor who suggested that they continue walking toward a group of farm buildings that lay ahead. Maybe someone there could give them directions—or even a ride to Petit Trianon.

It was strangely quiet as they headed down the wooded path. They soon reached a gate and saw two men working in the garden. The men were dressed oddly—in long grayish-green coats—and they seemed totally consumed with their work.

"Excuse me," Anne said in French. "Could one of you point me in the direction of Petit Trianon?"

Both men looked up, a little startled. "Do you plan to visit the Queen?" one asked, with a confused look on his face.

"Why, no, my dear. Whatever do you mean? Which queen? France no longer has royalty," Anne replied.

The men looked even more confused than ever and shook their heads.

"Come, Anne," Eleanor said. "These two gentlemen must be confused. Let's head toward the cottage and ask for help."

The two made their way to a cottage. In front of the small house, standing on steep stone steps, they saw a woman and a young girl. Both were wearing long dresses. Although the dresses were a bit tattered, they had once been beautiful. The fabric, Anne noticed, was exquisite.

"Excuse me," Anne began, only to be suddenly interrupted. From around the corner a strange man appeared, wearing a wide-brimmed hat and cloak. His dark-skinned face was badly marked by small, round scars.

"May I show you the way, mesdames?" the man asked and bowed with a flourish. He pointed to a bridge and a ravine. "The place you are searching for is just over there. You're almost there," he said, again bowing low to the two women.

The teachers headed off in the direction where he pointed, not knowing what to make of what they had just seen. It was as if they had stumbled onto some strange historical pageant, complete with people in costume.

But as they approached the building they recognized as Petit Trianon, things grew even stranger. Once again, the air was eerily still. Off in the distance, the two could see a couple of workers loading sticks into a cart. The workers were dressed oddly for such a task—in red and blue capes. The rest of Petit Trianon seemed deserted. Just to the right of the two men sat a woman, her hair white with powder. She was sketching the scene in front of her and seemed unaware of the presence of the two visitors.

Then, in the blink of an eye, the two teachers were back in their room at their hotel. The whole situation was incredibly weird. Neither of them could remember how they got back to Paris, nor did they know how much time had passed since their sightseeing trip had started.

But they both were certain they had been to the summer estate. And their tired limbs and muddy shoes were proof that they had walked some distance.

The incident haunted the two women. The next day, they went to the French Academy of History to see if they could get to the bottom of what had happened. There, they researched Petit Trianon and the surrounding areas.

Anne was shocked at what she found. The gray-green costume she had seen the first two men wearing matched the uniform of the royal livery during the time of Marie Antoinette. In another of the old dusty volumes, Eleanor found an article about the caretaker's cottage. It reported that a fourteen-year-old girl lived there with her mother, who was Marie Antoinette's cook in 1789.

Then there was some information about a

pock-marked man. According to one of the books they uncovered, Marie Antoinette had an intimate friend named the Comte de Vaudriuil. The reference said he was pock-marked and was of Creole descent, which would explain his dark skin.

Then they found the strangest coincidence of all. Marie Antoinette liked to spend her summer days sketching the fields of Petit Trianon. She usually did so completely alone, with no ladies at her side.

Had the two actually stepped back in time? Had they somehow slipped through history's window and actually become part of Marie Antoinette's world? Had they, in fact, actually seen Marie Antoinette? Or was this all some sort of strange coincidence? Perhaps there was some logical explanation. Perhaps, indeed, the Petit Trianon hosted some sort of historical programs that featured costumed participants. The women had to find out.

The next day, they headed back to Petit Trianon. When they arrived, they were shocked to find that the place was far different from the one they had seen previously. There were no farm buildings and no cottage. Only a fallen stone wall marked where a cottage once might have been. There was no ravine either, nor a bridge that led to Petit Trianon, only a well-worn pathway.

When the two approached the building, they were met by a caretaker, but he was far different from the cloaked gentleman they had seen earlier. He wore modern clothes and simple pants, and he behaved quite normally.

"Tell me, sir," Anne asked, "is Petit Trianon ever home to some sort of historical pageant with actors in costumes playing roles?"

The caretaker shook his head. "No," he replied. "We operate mostly as a simple museum. There's no budget for that kind of fancy show."

"Do you know," Eleanor continued, "if there was a small cottage just over that ravine?"

"And a bridge? Was there ever a bridge?" Anne asked.

The caretaker smiled. "Yes, how did you know? The cottage was home to Marie Antoinette's cook and her daughter, but it fell into disrepair years ago and was finally torn down.

"And there was a bridge, too," he continued. "It was part of the formal gardens the Queen had created in this part of her world. But it fell down many years ago."

Anne finally believed what she would not let herself believe before. She had indeed, somehow, slipped through time and had visited eighteenth-century France. And, as she wrote years later in a famous book about the incident, "I would not have believed such a thing could happen . . . but now I know that indeed all things are possible."

THE
ANGEL
OF
THE
BATTLEFIELD

*S*OME call them guardian angels, these spirit-
beings that seem to be sent from heaven to
protect us on earth. They don't always take the
form of a traditional angel, with wings and
flowing robes. Instead, they sometimes appear
as normal human beings. Occasionally, they
come strangely dressed, as if they have returned from a time in history. Some have even
appeared as young children.

But no matter what they look like, their

mission is always the same—to save the faithful from danger or certain death. And as one Civil War soldier discovered, they can overcome the most powerful forces in order to accomplish their missions of mercy.

The American Civil War was a bitter and bloody event, fought with Springfield rifles and bayonets. The battles often ended in hand-to-hand combat, fights in which neighbor was often pitted against neighbor, brother against brother. It was a war that tore our country apart, a war from which the United States would take years to recover.

This war divided not only the country, but families, too. The Bates family was one of those families. When Joshua Bates heard news of the war, he quickly signed up with the Confederate Army. He thought it was his duty to defend his Virginia homeland.

But Joshua's father, a Baptist minister, was dead set against it. War was the devil's work, he claimed, and this war was certainly the most evil of them all. When Joshua left to join his fellow Virginians on the battlefield, his father was furious. He claimed he would never speak to his son again. Even though Joshua's mother begged her husband to reconsider, she realized her husband was too stubborn to do any such thing. If Joshua survived the bloody battles ahead of him, she knew that she would probably never see her son again.

Joshua couldn't understand his father's feelings, but Joshua knew he couldn't change his father's mind. And Joshua also knew that he couldn't and wouldn't change his own mind about becoming a rebel soldier.

The battle in the Wilderness changed all of that. The Wilderness was a densely wooded forest in the Pennsylvania mountains. The vines and undergrowth were so thick that not one man—and certainly not an entire division of the Confederate Army—could move through. So on their journey north, Bates and the rest of the division planned to take a path known as the Orange Turnpike to bypass the tangled mess.

But Union General Ulysses S. Grant got wind of their plan. Moving quickly, he mobilized the Union forces under General Warren and surprised the Confederate division with an all-out attack. The attack turned into a battle that spread throughout the Wilderness itself. To Bates, it was a bloody mass of confusion. The battle lines became confused in the thick brush. Bates found himself simply firing his rifle into the bushes, thinking he might actually hit a Union soldier. Other soldiers did the same, firing at the enemy at point-blank range. Others slung their rifles over their shoulders and simply fought hand-to-hand or bayonet-to-bayonet. Many soldiers died. Thousands more were wounded. They fell into the thick underbrush and lay moaning for help, but they were not likely to be found.

And then the fires started. The rifle shots had started a few small fires in the dry leaves, and, as darkness fell, those small fires grew larger, until a raging forest fire spread across the Wilderness. Joshua feared the worst. Unless something was done quickly, the wounded were doomed to die a fiery death. Maybe his father had been right, he thought to himself. War *was* the devil's work.

As the night sky blazed with the fire, each army decided to call a truce. They would help each other recover their wounded before they burned to death in the Wilderness inferno.

Bates volunteered to head one of the rescue teams. He and three others advanced into the fiery blaze. They retrieved the soldiers they could and carried them back into the clearing along the Orange Turnpike. They saved as many as they could.

The site of the fire burning around him was bad enough, but the sound was even more terrible. The roar of the fire was almost drowned out by the screams of the men as the fire overtook them. Suddenly, Bates heard a wail right beside him. It was a wounded Union soldier.

"My legs! My legs!" he screamed. Bates looked down. The man's gray pants were on fire. Quickly, Bates grabbed handfuls of dirt and put it out. Then, coughing from the smoke, he carried the man from the blazing woods to the clearing. He left him there so others could tend to him, and Joshua headed back into the blaze once more.

He repeated his mission of mercy over and over, rescuing ten soldiers, both Confederate and Union. His comrades begged him to stop. They knew he was tired. The fire was burning so wildly that there could be no more survivors.

On their last trip into the inferno, they had heard no screams, only the roar of the blaze in their ears.

But Bates had to be sure that he had saved everyone that he could. "One more time," he gasped. "I'll just go in one more time."

Bates then turned and headed once again into the fire. This time he headed slightly south toward an area he had not searched before.

Then he heard it. "Help us! Please, God, help us!"

There, huddled underneath a rocky crag, were two soldiers. One had been wounded in his leg. The other seemed unhurt, but dazed, as if the horror of the battle and the fire that followed were too much for him to take.

"I'm here," Bates said to the men. "I'll get you out of here."

As Bates said those words, he heard a loud crack, followed by a crash. A huge tree fell just in front of the three of them, blocking their escape from the fire. They were trapped. There was no way out.

Joshua was sure they faced a fiery death. It would be only a matter of minutes before the the fire or the smoke would overtake them.

He thought back to his father and the angry words they had exchanged when he left home. How he wished he could take those words back. How he wished he could see his father again, just once more.

Joshua knew what his father would do in this situation—he would pray. And that's exactly what Joshua did. "We must pray," he said to the two soldiers. "We must pray for our salvation."

The three men joined hands and coughed and sputtered desperate prayers. Even as Joshua murmured the prayers, he prepared for the flames to engulf him.

Then, miraculously, the figure of a man appeared in front of the three soldiers. The man was neither Union or Confederate. In fact, he didn't appear as if he was a soldier at all. He was taller than the three men and wore a kind of brown sackcloth gown, almost like a monk would wear.

"Come," the man said in a gentle voice. "Follow me. I will show you the way out."

Incredulous, Joshua stood, then bent down and picked up the man with the wounded leg.

"Quickly, now," the man said in a calm but firm voice.

Joshua looked ahead to where the man was leading them. It was a wall of flame. They couldn't possibly pass through it, but Joshua knew he had no choice.

As the man in the brown robe headed into the fire, it was as if a powerful wind blew the flames apart. The four passed through a narrow pathway, with flames leaping on either side. Looking back, Joshua saw the flames converge as the path closed after them.

Joshua's heart pounded as the men reached the clearing. He was quickly surrounded by his fellow soldiers, all cheering him for his heroic act. The two other men were taken to be treated with the other wounded men. They would live, thanks to Joshua, his commander told him.

"But it wasn't only me," Joshua insisted. "I had help. A monk helped show me the way. There must be a monastery or something a-round here someplace."

"A monastery? In these parts?" His com-mander laughed. "I think not. Don't be so modest, Bates. There was no one else. You saved those two men yourself and you deserve the credit."

"You're wrong. He must still be around here. He showed us the way out."

Joshua searched in vain for the man who had saved him, but he couldn't find him at the camp. And, as he reviewed the whole incident in his mind, it had seemed so strange—the tall man, the strange clothes, the way the fire had seemed to part to let them through.

Joshua puzzled over the incident for the rest of the war. When the Southern forces finally surrendered, he headed back to his family's place in Virginia. He didn't know what he would find there. Would his home still be standing? Would his family all be safe? And, if all else was well, would his father ever forgive him? Now that he had faced death, he realized the importance of life and love for one's family. He couldn't waste any more time on an old grudge.

As he walked down the path to his family's house, he could see the red rooftop shining in the sunlight. His house was still there! He breathed a sigh of relief, then swallowed hard again. Now if only his father could have a change of heart.

He knocked on the door, his hand shaking

a bit with anticipation. His father answered, and a small smile spread upon his face the moment he saw Joshua. Words were not needed. Joshua knew he had been forgiven.

Joshua and his parents talked long into the evening, discussing the war in horrific detail. Joshua left out much of it—especially the part about the dangerous fire. He didn't want to upset his mother.

When his mother finally went to bed, Joshua began telling more of the war's horror stories to his father.

"Tell me, Son," his father asked, "of all of the dangers you faced, was fire among them?"

Joshua felt his heart race. "Yes, Father, a terrible fire after a bloody battle. Many of the wounded burned where they fell. I tried to save as many as I could . . .," he said, his voice choking with emotion. "Father," he said, "how did you know?"

His father sighed. "I dreamt of it, Son. Of a horrible fire and of you trying to save your fellow men. And after that dream, I woke up and prayed with all of my might. I prayed to God to send an angel to help you. I knew that without that help, you should surely die."

Joshua thought back to the fire and the mysterious stranger in the brown robe.

Now he knew why he had never seen the stranger again. Joshua knew it was an angel who had saved his life and who made it possible for Joshua and his father to forgive and go on.

About The Author

There is nothing Tracey Dils likes better than a good ghost story. When she was growing up, she loved to scare her friends and family with terrifying tales of haunted places. In fact, she scared her little sister so badly that to this day she still sleeps with the lights on!

Ms. Dils has never actually seen a ghost, but she has seen evidence of one. She was having lunch at an old inn in her hometown. The inn was said to be haunted. While she was eating, a tray of salt and pepper shakers rose off a counter, hung in midair for a few seconds, and then fell to the floor in one big crash. She thinks a ghost was trying to get her attention so that she'd write a story about it.

When she's not writing or spending time with her husband, Richard, and her two children, Emily and Phillip, Ms. Dils loves to talk to young people about writing. She has held ghost-story writing workshops in schools, libraries, and writing centers throughout her home state.

Ms. Dils is also the author of *Real-life Scary Places*, *Real-life Scary Kids*, and *The Scariest Stories You've Ever Heard, Part III*. She has also written several picture books, including *Annabelle's Awful Waffle*, *A Look Around Coral Reefs*, *Big Bad Bugs*, and *Leapin' Lizards*.